Discovering Savannah

Uncovering 100+ Local Gems, Iconic Landmarks and Culinary Delights

Susyn S. Shepherd

While every precaution has been taken in the preparation of this book, the publisher assumes no responsibility for errors or omissions, or for damages resulting from the use of the information contained herein.

DISCOVERING SAVANNAH

First edition. August 5, 2023.

ISBN: 979-8223729204

Written by Susyn S. Shepherd.

Table of Contents

Preface

Welcome, dear friend, to the enchanting world of Savannah, Georgia, a city that holds a special place in my heart. Over the past two decades, I've visited Savannah and Tybee Island more times than I can count, and each trip feels like a homecoming. This city's tremendous energy, steeped in history and brimming with cultural events, has woven its magic into me, making it my go-to vacation spot.

You see, Savannah, GA, isn't just any destination for me; it's a cherished retreat that calls me back time and time again. The moment I set foot on its cobblestone streets, I felt an immediate connection to the warm embrace of Southern hospitality. Whether wandering through the historic squares or indulging in mouthwatering culinary delights along River Street, the sense of belonging washes over me like a familiar melody.

But what truly makes Savannah extraordinary is its passion for its visitors—including our four-legged companions! This dog-friendly city has welcomed my furry friends with open arms, allowing us to create cherished memories together. The joy of exploring the charming squares, strolling along River Street, and sharing laughter at the lively festivals is an experience I cherish beyond words.

As I've delved deeper into the soul of Savannah to create this guide, it has been a labor of love. Unraveling its history, discovering hidden gems, and indulging in delectable treats have only intensified my affection for this incredible area nestled on the coast of South Georgia. And now, I'm delighted to share my insights and insider tips as if I were your expert travel and food writer guide, here to unveil the wonders of Savannah, Georgia, just like I would with a dear friend.

So, let's embark on this journey together as I share the stories and treasures that make Savannah so extraordinary. From its historic landmarks to the lively festivals, from the serenity of the islands to the delicious flavors that linger on the taste buds, we'll explore it all. I hope this guide brings you as much joy and excitement as it has brought me in creating it.

Ah, and don't let me forget to mention that Savannah is the ultimate destination to check off some of those bucket list items too! It's a city that can turn your travel dreams into reality. Savannah has everything, whether you've always yearned to stroll through historic districts filled with architectural wonders, indulge in the finest coastal cuisine, go dolphin watching, or see a sunset on a beautiful island retreat.

With its rich history and cultural heritage, this charming city offers you the chance to immerse yourself in experiences you've only dreamed of. From exploring the iconic Forsyth Park to reliving Civil War history at Fort Pulaski, each moment is an opportunity to cross off those cherished items from your bucket list.

And let's not forget the islands! Tybee Island's sandy beaches and Skidaway Island State Park's natural trails provide the perfect backdrop for outdoor adventures, bringing you closer to the untouched beauty of the South.

Oh, and if you're an animal lover like me, Savannah won't disappoint! The Oatland Island Wildlife Center and Dolphin Watching Tours are just a few excursions offering unique encounters with fascinating wildlife, making it a dream come true for those who've always wanted to connect with nature.

With every step you take and every bite you savor, Savannah offers you the chance to embrace life to the fullest, to cross off those bucket list activities with a smile on your face. So whether you're an avid history buff, a culinary enthusiast, or a nature lover seeking thrilling adventures, Savannah welcomes you with open arms to embark on the journey of a lifetime.

As you delve into this guide, my dear friend, I hope you find inspiration and excitement in the diverse array of experiences Savannah offers. So let's make this trip one for the books, checking off those personal bucket list activities individually and creating unforgettable memories that will stay with us forever.

So buckle up, my friend, as we dive into the captivating world of Savannah. This city holds the power to enchant, captivate, and leave an indelible mark on your heart. Welcome to my beloved Savannah, where every visit feels like coming home. Let's enjoy every moment, cherish every experience, and create memories that will last a lifetime. Have a great time in Savannah!

Introduction

Hey there, fellow adventurers! Welcome to Savannah, Georgia's charming, soulful city – where Southern hospitality and fascinating history come together for an unforgettable experience! I'll be your trusty travel and food writer guide, ready to show you the best-kept secrets, hidden gems, and must-visit landmarks that Savannah offers.

Nestled along the banks of the Savannah River and adorned with cobblestone streets, this enchanting city has a timeless appeal that draws visitors from near and far. With its stunning architecture, historic squares draped in Spanish moss, and a lively arts scene, Savannah is filled with an amazingly diverse range of experiences waiting to be explored.

The Purpose of this Book: Your Ultimate Savannah Bucket List

Now, you might wonder what this book is all about. Well, my dear wanderers, the purpose is simple – to guide you on your ultimate Savannah bucket list experience. Whether you're a first-time visitor eager to uncover the city's iconic landmarks or a seasoned traveler searching for hidden gems, this book has something for everyone. From historical treasures to culinary delights, from island escapades to lively nightlife, Savannah's offerings are as diverse as they are delightful.

In this book, we're going to embark on an extraordinary journey through the heart and soul of Savannah. Picture yourself strolling through enchanting squares and gazing up at stunning architectural wonders found all throughout Savannah's Historic District – it's like stepping back in time, y'all!

How to Use this Book: Unravel the City's Enchanting Tapestry

Diving into the chapters of this book will be like unraveling the beautiful tapestry that makes up Savannah's allure. Picture yourself walking through the city's historic squares, where each one has its own story to tell. Imagine savoring mouthwatering Southern cuisine in charming eateries recommended by locals who know the city's culinary pulse like the back of their hand. Visualize setting sail to Savannah's nearby islands, where sandy beaches, coastal vistas, and wildlife encounters await.

Each chapter will be your gateway to a different aspect of Savannah, offering insider tips, intriguing facts, and personal recommendations that only a seasoned traveler can provide. You'll be introduced to the city's interesting history, from Revolutionary War to Civil War, from various landmarks to tales of haunted spots and famous pirate legends. You can find all of that here.

So, pack your sense of adventure, curiosity, and an empty stomach ready to be filled with great-tasting food because Savannah is about to reveal its many layers of charm and magic. From historic homes to hidden alleys, from ghost tours to sunny beaches, your Savannah bucket list adventure awaits. Join me as we explore this fascinating city, uncovering its treasures and making memories to last for generations to come.

Get ready for an unforgettable journey through Savannah, Georgia – the epitome of Southern charm and hospitality! Get excited, get curious, and get ready to fall in love. This vibrant city welcomes you with an interesting mix of old-world charm and modern attractions. So, let's start knocking off a few of those bucket list items. Alright, enough chit-chat – let's go!

Chapter 1

Embrace Savannah's Historic Treasures

Hey there, my fellow adventurers! It's time to delve into the heart of Savannah's intricate past with a journey through its historic treasures. As we venture into Savannah's Historic District, prepare to step into a time machine. Beautiful squares and stunning architecture take the stage in this setting. It's like walking through a living history book!

As we explore Savannah's historic treasures, we will enter an era of timeless beauty and warm Southern hospitality. In this chapter, we'll wander through the enchanting squares and architectural wonders that make Savannah a city like no other. But before we delve into the history, let's talk about the essence of Southern hospitality that infuses every corner of this gracious city.

The captivating charm of must-see historic homes like the Mercer-Williams House and Owens-Thomas House will carry you back to a bygone time, from the awe-inspiring Historic District, embellished with 22 lovely squares and architectural treasures. Every aspect of this district has a story to tell, from the majestic grandeur of Forsyth Park to the anecdotes spoken by the moss-covered tombstones at Bonaventure Cemetery.

Did You Know? A network of mysterious underground tunnels, known as "vaults" or "catacombs," is snaking their way beneath some of the city's squares. These hidden passages have stood the test of time, connecting historic buildings and serving various purposes throughout history. From secretive storage spaces to clandestine passageways, these vaults have witnessed the city's evolution and tales of old.

Savannah's reputation for Southern hospitality is as legendary as its cobblestone streets and Spanish moss-draped oaks. From the moment you set foot in this charming city, you'll feel a genuine warmth that extends from the locals and echoes through the historic buildings. The inviting smiles and friendly greetings will make you feel like you've returned to a place where time slows down and connections with others are cherished.

Savannahians take great pride in sharing their city's stories, traditions, and cherished spots with visitors, ensuring you experience Southern grace's true essence. As we explore Savannah's historic district and its must-visit homes, cemeteries, and forts, you'll find that the city's past and present are woven into a tapestry of beauty, culture, and heartfelt hospitality.

And let's not forget about the jaw-dropping historic homes and haunted history passed along from generation to generation! If you're a history buff like me, get ready to be wowed by the grandeur of the Mercer-Williams House and Owens-Thomas House. These historic homes are a true feast for the eyes!

Let the adventure begin, without any more delay. Savannah is waiting for you with open arms and a rich history of wonderful adventures. Allow us to lead you through the magic of Savannah, Georgia. This city has the capacity to steal your heart and leave an indelible mark on your soul. Enjoy your journey!

We encourage you to check out:

Savannah's Historic District: Stroll through enchanting squares and architecture.

Welcome to the beating heart of Savannah – the Historic District! This is where the city's history comes alive with its 22 picturesque squares, each offering a unique charm and story. Take a leisurely walk under moss-draped oak trees and over cobblestone streets, admire the ornate ironwork on historic buildings, and soak in the Southern ambiance that fills the air. You'll find everything from serene gardens to lively fountains, making this district an actual open-air museum of beauty and history.

Did You Know? While Savannah's Historic District is famous for its stunning squares and historic homes, there's a fascinating secret hidden beneath the city's cobblestone streets. A network of underground tunnels, known as "vaults" or "catacombs," runs beneath some of the squares, connecting historic buildings and serving various purposes throughout history.

These tunnels were initially used for storage, providing easy access for merchants to transport goods without interrupting the picturesque street scene above. During the prohibition era, some of these tunnels gained notoriety as secret passageways for bootleggers and smugglers, making them an intriguing part of Savannah's storied past. While not all tunnels are accessible to the public, local legends and tour guides often share tales of these mysterious underground passageways during ghost and historical walking tours.

The Historic District's ageless charm never fades, no matter the season. Its cobblestone streets and elegant architecture create a charming backdrop for romantic carriage rides and leisurely walks. As you explore the district, pop into local boutiques and art galleries, showcasing the work of talented Savannah artists. Make time to visit the Historic Savannah Theatre, the oldest continually operating theater in the U.S., where you can catch lively performances year-round.

So, my fellow adventurers, whether you're chasing the vibrant blooms of spring, embracing the Southern charm of summer, enjoying the colorful splendor of fall, or basking in the holiday magic of winter, the Historic District has something interesting to offer in every season. Get ready to experience Savannah's beauty all year long and immerse yourself in its timeless charm!

Must-Visit Historic Homes: Experience the grandeur of the Mercer-Williams House and Owens-Thomas House.

Step into the luxury of two of Savannah's most iconic historic homes. The Mercer-Williams House, located at 429 Bull St, Savannah, GA 31401, is a striking mansion featured prominently in the novel "Midnight in the Garden of Good and Evil." Its exquisite architecture and lavish interiors offer a glimpse into Savannah's elite society.

There's more to discover beyond its lavish interiors when visiting the Mercer-Williams House. The house gained international attention when it became the backdrop for a murder trial. Are you familiar with the bestselling novel, "Midnight in the Garden of Good and Evil?" That's the one they are referring to.

The infamous trial of Jim Williams, a wealthy antique dealer accused of murder, drew crowds of curious onlookers to the house during the 1980s. Today, visitors can take guided tours to explore the luxurious rooms where the event unfolded and learn about the house's connection to the captivating true-crime story that continues to captivate readers and visitors alike.

Next is the Owens-Thomas House, located at 124 Abercorn St, Savannah, GA 31401. It is a true architectural gem. Designed by William Jay, this Federal-style masterpiece boasts stunning period furnishings and a unique indoor plumbing system that was way ahead of its time. Prepare to be transported back in time as you explore its vast halls and stunning gardens.

Insider's Tip: While the Owens-Thomas House is renowned for its architectural beauty, it also holds an unexpected treasure beneath its floors. The Owens-Thomas House is home to one of the earliest indoor plumbing systems in the United States, a revolutionary feature during the 19th century.

As you wander through the house, look for the hidden water cisterns and early flushing toilets that showcase the house's innovative and sophisticated design. It's a testament to the forward-thinking nature of Savannah's early architects and an intriguing insight into the technological advancements of the time.

Don't Miss the Bonaventure Cemetery: A hauntingly beautiful journey among moss-covered tombstones.

I know what you're thinking — a cemetery on a bucket list? But trust me, Bonaventure Cemetery is not your average spooky graveyard. It's hauntingly beautiful, moss-covered, and full of heartfelt stories.

Bonaventure Cemetery is unlike any other you've seen. Located at 330 Bonaventure Rd, Savannah, GA 31404, this hauntingly beautiful burial ground is an actual work of art. Ancient oak trees draped with Spanish moss cast a romantic veil over moss-covered tombstones, creating a serene and ethereal atmosphere. Take a guided tour or wander the paths, and you'll discover stunning sculptures, mausoleums, and memorials telling stories of the city's past residents.

If you're a fan of literature and poetry, Bonaventure Cemetery has a special connection to one of America's most celebrated poets, Conrad Aiken. Born in Savannah, Aiken spent his formative years near the cemetery, and the tranquility and beauty of this final resting place inspired much of his work. One of his most renowned poems, "Bonaventure," pays tribute to the cemetery's serene landscape and the timeless allure of Savannah.

Did You Know? Beyond its hauntingly beautiful façade, Bonaventure Cemetery holds a hidden legacy of art and symbolism. Many of the intricate gravestones and sculptures within the cemetery tell unique stories about the lives of those laid to rest. One fascinating aspect is the prevalence of "grave symbolism," where intricate carvings and tombstone designs carry specific meanings.

For example, you might come across angels representing a spiritual guide to the afterlife or broken columns symbolizing a life cut short. As you wander among the moss-covered tombstones, look closer at the artistry and symbolism etched into each monument, revealing heartfelt messages and the cultural expressions of Savannah's diverse community.

Fort Pulaski National Monument: Relive Civil War history at this well-preserved fort.

History buffs, this one's for you! Fort Pulaski National Monument is a must-visit. Step back in time to the Civil War era at Fort Pulaski National Monument, located at U.S. Hwy 80, Savannah, GA 31410. This formidable coastal fort played a significant role during the Civil War. It showcased the advances in military engineering of its time.

Explore the fort's various sections, climb atop its walls for scenic views, and witness thrilling cannon firings during demonstrations. It's an educational and immersive experience that brings the past to life. Trust me; you'll feel like you're right in the middle of the Civil War action with cannon firings and everything – it's epic!

DISCOVERING SAVANNAH

While Fort Pulaski is famous for its military history, it's also a wildlife haven teeming with diverse ecosystems. The fort is situated within the Savannah National Wildlife Refuge, which encompasses a vast salt marsh and tidal creeks. Nature enthusiasts should keep an eye out for resident and migratory bird species, such as herons, egrets, and raptors, as they soar above the marshlands.

Additionally, you might spot the elusive American alligator gliding through the waters or catch a glimpse of the endangered wood stork making a graceful appearance. Fort Pulaski truly offers a unique blend of history and nature, allowing visitors to appreciate the fort's military significance and the ecological wonders surrounding it.

So, keep these insider tips in mind to enrich your experience and gain a deeper appreciation for the hidden layers of history, art, and nature that make these iconic sites so extraordinary. Savannah's treasures are waiting to be discovered, and there's no better way to experience the city's charm than by embracing its mysteries and secret tales. Happy exploring!

Chapter 2

40+ Bucket List Places to Visit in Savannah, GA

Alright, y'all, hold onto your hats because we're about to dive head-first into the ultimate Savannah bucket list! We've covered everything, from the iconic landmarks you simply can't miss to some hidden gems that even locals adore. How many of these can you visit while you're here?

Picture this – Forsyth Park, where you can relax under ancient oak trees and soak in the beauty of the iconic fountain. And what about River Street, with its cobblestone charm and endless rows of shops and eateries? It's a paradise for the shopaholics and foodies among us!

But wait, there's more! How about exploring the artsy side of Savannah at the SCAD Museum of Art or taking a leisurely stroll along the enchanting Wormsloe Historic Site's Oak Avenue? Trust me, these spots will leave you feeling like you're in a fairytale.

Welcome to the heart and soul of Savannah, where every street corner holds a treasure waiting to be discovered. In this chapter, we'll explore an array of over 40 iconic landmarks, historic homes, and captivating island excursions that showcase the city's rich heritage and natural beauty. You'll undoubtedly want to visit as many of these as you can.

As you uncover Savannah's diverse treasures, you'll be captivated by the city's unique blend of history, culture, and natural wonders. From iconic landmarks to hidden gems, each stop on this journey offers a glimpse into the soul of Savannah, where the past and present seamlessly intertwine. So, get ready to embrace the spirit of exploration and embark on a memorable adventure through this enchanting city!

So let's get started.

2.1 Forsyth Park (Drayton St, Savannah, GA 31401): This beloved urban oasis is a must-visit for locals and visitors. Stroll under the majestic oaks, check out the iconic fountain at its center, and immerse yourself in this dog-friendly garden's aromatic blooms. Forsyth Park hosts events and festivals throughout the year, offering a lively atmosphere for everyone and it's free to enjoy.

2.2 River Street (River St, Savannah, GA 31401): Experience the old-world charm of Savannah's historic cobblestone street called River Street. Lined with boutiques, shops, and eateries, this bustling waterfront area offers stunning views of the Savannah River. It is the perfect place for a leisurely walk along the water's edge.

2.3 City Market (Bryan St, Savannah, GA 31401): Discover the beating heart of Savannah's downtown scene at City Market. This vibrant open-air marketplace features art galleries, boutiques, and various dining options. It's the perfect spot to shop for unique souvenirs and indulge in some local flavors.

2.4 Cathedral of St. John the Baptist (222 E Harris St, Savannah, GA 31401): Prepare to be awe-struck by the grandeur of the Cathedral of St. John the Baptist. Its stunning Gothic architecture, intricate artwork, and impressive stained glass windows are one of those things that you shouldn't miss, especially for architecture and history enthusiasts.

2.5 Savannah History Museum (303 Martin Luther King Jr Blvd, Savannah, GA 31401): Dive into Savannah's captivating past at the Savannah History Museum. Interactive exhibits and fascinating artifacts offer a glimpse into the city's unique heritage, from its colonial beginnings to the modern era.

2.6 Old Fort Jackson (Fort Jackson Rd, Savannah, GA 31404): Travel back in time to the Civil War era at Old Fort Jackson. This well-preserved fort allows you to witness cannon firings, explore historical exhibits, and enjoy panoramic views of the Savannah River.

2.7 The Pirate's House (20 E Broad St, Savannah, GA 31401): Step into the pages of history at The Pirate's House, a restaurant with a colorful pirate history dating back to the 1700s. Enjoy lunch at this historic restaurant while learning about the city's seafaring tales and ghostly stories.

2.8 Mercer Williams House Museum (429 Bull St, Savannah, GA 31401): As the setting of the book "Midnight in the Garden of Good and Evil," the Mercer Williams House Museum holds both historical significance and literary allure. Explore its opulent interiors and hear stories about the intriguing characters who once graced its halls.

2.9 Davenport House Museum (323 E Broughton St, Savannah, GA 31401): Step into the early 19th century at the Davenport House Museum. This well-preserved historic home offers a glimpse into daily life during Savannah's formative years and showcases the city's architectural heritage.

2.10 Juliette Gordon Low Birthplace (10 E Oglethorpe Ave, Savannah, GA 31401): Delve into the inspiring story of the founder of Girl Scouts USA at the Juliette Gordon Low Birthplace. Filled with personal artifacts and interactive exhibits, this museum honors the life and legacy of this remarkable woman.

2.11 Ships of the Sea Maritime Museum (41 Martin Luther King Jr Blvd, Savannah, GA 31401): Explore Savannah's maritime history at the Ships of the Sea Maritime Museum. View amazing ship models, navigational instruments, and exhibitions that highlight the city's significance in the maritime industry.

2.12 Savannah African Art Museum (201 E 37th St, Savannah, GA 31401): At the Savannah African Art Museum, you may immerse yourself in Africa's rich culture. This intimate museum houses an impressive African art and artifacts collection, providing every visitor a unique and enriching experience.

2.13 Telfair Museums (207 W York St, Savannah, GA 31401): Comprising three museums – the Telfair Academy, Jepson Center, and Owens-Thomas House & Slave Quarters – the Telfair Museums offer a diverse range of artistic and historical experiences. You can admire fine art, delve into contemporary exhibits, and learn about Savannah's complex past.

2.14 Massie Heritage Center (207 E Gordon St, Savannah, GA 31401): Delve into the heart of Savannah's history, architecture, and culture at the Massie Heritage Center. Interactive exhibits and educational programs offer a dynamic exploration of the city's heritage.

2.15 SCAD Museum of Art (601 Turner Blvd, Savannah, GA 31401): Art enthusiasts will be captivated by the SCAD Museum of Art. As part of the Savannah College of Art and Design, this contemporary art museum showcases works by emerging and established artists, providing a fresh and innovative perspective on the art world.

2.16 Lafayette Square (Abercorn St, Savannah, GA 31401): One of Savannah's most charming squares, Lafayette Square exudes a sense of tranquility. Surrounded by historic buildings and adorned with a striking statue of Lafayette, it offers a peaceful oasis for relaxation and contemplation.

2.17 Ellis Square (Barnard St, Savannah, GA 31401): Ellis Square is a lively and inviting public space featuring a playground, interactive fountain, and various restaurants. It's the perfect spot to take a break, soak up the vibrant atmosphere, and enjoy a refreshing beverage under the shade trees.

2.18 Chippewa Square (Bull St, Savannah, GA 31401): Film buffs will recognize Chippewa Square as the iconic location where Forrest Gump sat on a bench recounting his life's adventures. As you stroll through this square, you can't help but reminisce about the beloved movie and its timeless quotes.

2.19 Johnson Square (Bull St, Savannah, GA 31401): Johnson Square is steeped in history as the oldest and largest square in Savannah. The towering Christ Church stands at its center, offering a sense of spiritual serenity amidst the bustling cityscape.

2.20 Whitefield Square (Habersham St, Savannah, GA 31401): Escape to Whitefield Square's peaceful environment, where a gorgeous gazebo and inviting benches invite you to relax. Surrounded by beautiful homes, this square is a hidden gem that captures the essence of Savannah's elegance.

2.21 Green-Meldrim House (14 W Macon St, Savannah, GA 31401): This National Historic Landmark holds a fascinating Civil War history. It served as the residence of General William T. Sherman during his occupation of Savannah. You can also take a guided tour of the Green-Meldrim House to uncover its role in shaping the city's past.

2.22 Andrew Low House (329 Abercorn St, Savannah, GA 31401): A visit to the Andrew Low House transports you back to Savannah's antebellum era. Admire the rich interiors and take a stroll through the impressive garden, which remains a calm oasis in the center of the city.

2.23 Wormsloe Historic Site (7601 Skidaway Rd, Savannah, GA 31406): An enchanting avenue of beautiful live oak trees welcomes you to Wormsloe Historic Site. Explore the ruins of a colonial estate, walk the nature trails, and discover the compelling history of Georgia's early settlers.

2.24 Owens-Thomas House & Slave Quarters (124 Abercorn St, Savannah, GA 31401): Beyond the luxury of the Owens-Thomas House lies a significant piece of history – the preserved slave quarters. Gain insights into the lives of those who toiled on the property and learn more about their contributions to Savannah's development.

2.25 Colonial Park Cemetery (200 Abercorn St, Savannah, GA 31401): Explore the atmospheric Colonial Park Cemetery, which is home to some of Savannah's first settlers. Fascinating gravestones tell stories of the past, and some visitors claim to have encountered ghostly apparitions during guided ghost tours.

2.26 The Beach Institute (502 E Harris St, Savannah, GA 31401): A hidden gem dedicated to African American history and art, The Beach Institute honors the contributions of Savannah's African American community. Engaging exhibits and cultural programs provide a deeper understanding of the city's diverse heritage.

2.27 Independent Presbyterian Church (207 Bull St, Savannah, GA 31401): Stand in awe of the striking Gothic architecture of the Independent Presbyterian Church. As one of the city's prominent landmarks, this majestic church offers a glimpse into Savannah's religious heritage.

2.28 Savannah Theatre (222 Bull St, Savannah, GA 31401): Experience the magic of live performances at the Savannah Theatre, the oldest continuously operating theater in the United States. From musicals to comedy shows, this historic venue offers top-notch entertainment year-round for all ages.

2.29 Roundhouse Railroad Museum (655 Louisville Rd, Savannah, GA 31401): Delve into Savannah's railroad history at the Roundhouse Railroad Museum. Explore vintage locomotives, view model trains, and learn about the pivotal role of railroads in shaping the city's growth.

2.30 Harper Fowlkes House (230 Barnard St, Savannah, GA 31401): Step into the past at the meticulously restored Harper Fowlkes House. Its beautiful gardens and elegant interiors provide a glimpse into Savannah's aristocratic life during the 19th century.

2.31 Andrew Low Carriage House (329 Abercorn St, Savannah, GA 31401): Adjacent to the Andrew Low House, the Carriage House dives into the life and contributions of Juliette Gordon Low, the founder of Girl Scouts USA.

2.32 Sorrel-Weed House (6 W Harris St, Savannah, GA 31401): For those seeking a taste of the supernatural, the Sorrel-Weed House is rumored to be haunted, making it a popular destination for ghost tours. If you dare, step inside this historic home and explore its spooky legends and eerie atmosphere.

2.33 Talmadge Memorial Bridge: Take a leisurely stroll along the Talmadge Memorial Bridge for breathtaking views of Savannah's skyline and the majestic Savannah River. Walking across this iconic bridge, you'll be treated to stunning panoramas that showcase the city's modern charm.

2.34 Isle of Hope (Isle of Hope Historic District, Savannah, GA 31406): Venture to the picturesque Isle of Hope, a riverside neighborhood steeped in history and natural beauty. Explore the quaint streets lined with historic homes and immerse yourself in the peaceful ambiance of this charming community.

2.35 Savannah National Wildlife Refuge: (694 Beech Hill Lane, Hardeeville, SC 29927): The Savannah National Wildlife Refuge, located between Georgia and South Carolina, is sure to please nature lovers. This vast sanctuary provides a haven for a wide variety of bird species and chances for wildlife photography and birding.

2.36 Wet Willie's (101 E River Street, Savannah, GA 31401): At Wet Willie's, adults of drinking age can take in Savannah's seaside charm while enjoying handcrafted frozen daiquiris in many unique flavors. Wet Willie's is a popular must-visit for hungry or thirsty tourists as well as locals.

2.37 Temple Mickve Israel (20 E Gordon St, Savannah, GA 31401): One of the oldest synagogues in America, Temple Mickve Israel showcases stunning Gothic-style architecture. Explore the vibrant history of Savannah's Jewish community and the enduring legacy of this cherished place of worship.

2.38 The Pirates' House Herb House (20 E Broad St, Savannah, GA 31401): Uncover a hidden gem within The Pirates' House as you explore the charming Herb House, the oldest house in Georgia. Guided tours and unique gifts make this off-the-beaten-path location a delightful find for curious travelers.

2.39 Juliette Gordon Low's Bedroom (10 E Oglethorpe Ave, Savannah, GA 31401): Step inside the intimate world of Juliette Gordon Low, the visionary founder of the Girl Scouts, as you explore her bedroom. Personal touches and memorabilia tell the story of her inspiring journey and the lasting impact of the organization she founded.

2.40 Savannah Cotton Exchange (201 E River St, Savannah, GA 31401): A historic building with an impressive cast-iron façade, the Savannah Cotton Exchange serves as a reminder of the city's past as a thriving cotton port. Admire the architectural details and imagine the bustling trade that once took place within these walls.

Island Excursions:

2.41 Wassaw Island: Venture to Wassaw Island, an untouched barrier island accessible only by boat. As a pristine wilderness area, this secluded island offers unspoiled beaches and diverse wildlife, making it a nature lover's paradise.

2.42 Little Tybee Island: Escape the crowds and explore the tranquil shores of Little Tybee Island. This undiscovered treasure offers a tranquil and serene break from the hectic pace of the city, with its peaceful beaches, tidal creeks, and chances for outdoor exploration and birdwatching.

2.43 Skidaway Island State Park (52 Diamond Causeway, Savannah, GA 31411): Skidaway Island State Park is a haven for nature lovers. This park displays the beauty of Georgia's coastal landscape with its hiking paths, marshland vistas, and educational information center.

2.44 Cockspur Island Lighthouse (Cockspur Island, Savannah, GA 31410): Embark on a boat tour to visit the historic Cockspur Island Lighthouse near the Savannah River entrance. This iconic landmark offers a glimpse into Savannah's maritime past.

2.45 Lazaretto Creek: Take a captivating boat tour along Lazaretto Creek, where you can explore the marshes, spot dolphins frolicking in the waters, and visit the picturesque Cockspur Island with its historic lighthouse.

Bonus: Hidden Gems

So you've seen Savannah's historical sites and enjoyed a few tasty treats on River Street. Now, let me take you on a small detour through a few lesser-known treasures that even seasoned visitors may need to uncover.

2.46 Savannah's Secret Gardens: Did you know that Savannah is a city teeming with enchanting secret gardens? Sneak away to the Washington Square Garden, nestled away from the bustling streets, offering a peaceful haven to sit back and embrace the charm of blooming flowers and towering oak trees. If you're searching for solitude and an oasis of greenery, head over to the Whitefield Square Garden, tucked away from the main tourist routes, perfect for a peaceful afternoon escape. Lastly, tucked-away oases like the Trustees' Garden, hidden behind a historic brick wall is a place where locals love to unwind with a good book or a leisurely picnic. These hidden green havens are perfect for moments of serenity amidst the city's vibrant energy.

2.47 Eclectic Antiques and Art Galleries: Beyond the well-known historic homes and museums, Savannah is an art lover's paradise with hidden art galleries and antique shops. Delve into the world of eccentric creations, avant-garde masterpieces, and quirky sculptures that challenge convention and ignite your imagination. You'll be amazed by the ingenuity of Savannah's local artists and the one-of-a-kind pieces they produce. Wander through the Starland District, where artistic expression oozes from every corner, with galleries showcasing innovative works from local talents. For antique enthusiasts, the Design District is a vintage finder's paradise that will transport you back in time. So, if you want to add a touch of uniqueness to your home decor or appreciate art in its many diverse forms, these hidden gems have got you covered!

2.48 Tales of Hauntings and Mysteries: Now I know Savannah is famous for its spooky tales, but there's more to it than just the ghost tours on River Street. Locals swear by the eerie stories surrounding places like the Sorrel-Weed House, rumored to be haunted by restless spirits. Explore lesser-known ghost tours, such as the Bonaventure Cemetery after dark, where scary legends come to life amid the spooky atmosphere. If you're up for a thrilling adventure and a chance to feel a shiver down your spine, these lesser-known haunts are a must-visit.

2.49 Hidden Culinary Gems: Beyond the renowned dining spots, some real culinary treasures are hiding in Savannah's nooks and crannies. Venture to the Victorian District, and you'll stumble upon cozy eateries serving up delectable dishes that the locals swear by. From soul-soothing comfort foods to exotic flavors from faraway lands, these hidden gems are a treat for your taste buds. So, follow your nose and indulge in these culinary secrets, and trust me, your foodie soul will thank you!

2.50 Artistic Alleyways: While many travelers stick to the main streets, Savannah's charm also lies in its artistic alleyways, each with a unique personality of its own. Wander through the Jones Street Alley, adorned with colorful murals that bring an extra splash of vibrancy to the city's canvas. And don't forget to explore the Factors Walk, where you'll find charming hidden shops and art installations tucked away along the riverfront. These artistic oases are perfect for those seeking inspiration and a glimpse into the city's creative spirit.

2.51 Underground Speakeasy Vibes: Remember those hidden catacombs we talked about earlier? Well, some of them hold another little secret - speakeasy-style bars! These swanky and secretive spots are perfect for an evening of craft cocktails and good company. Unwind in dimly lit, Prohibition-era atmospheres, sipping on carefully curated concoctions that will transport you back in time.

2.52 Secret Rooftop Retreats: Escape the hustle and bustle of the city streets and head upwards to Savannah's secret rooftop retreats. These exclusive spots offer breathtaking views of the city's skyline and a chance to unwind in a private oasis. Whether looking for a chic rooftop lounge or a cozy hidden terrace, these lofty gems are perfect for romantic moments and unforgettable sunsets. It's a unique experience that only a few visitors know about, but trust me, it's well worth the climb!

2.53 Midnight Cemetery Tours: Get ready for a spooky adventure! After the sun sets, some local guides offer midnight cemetery tours that take you deep into Savannah's haunted history. Stroll among ancient tombstones, listen to eerie ghost tales, and embrace the eerie atmosphere of these hallowed grounds. If you're feeling brave, this is definitely an experience you will remember!

2.54 Underground Jazz Joints: Dive into Savannah's soulful musical roots at the city's underground jazz joints. Follow the distant sounds of smooth melodies and toe-tapping rhythms to discover intimate venues where local jazz musicians showcase their talent. It's the perfect spot to unwind, mingle with the locals, and let the music carry you away.

2.55 Starland District: The Artsy Enclave: Nestled away from the touristy hustle, the Starland District is where the locals flock for arts, culture, and eclectic vibes. Stroll through this bohemian enclave and find vibrant street art, indie boutiques, and charming cafes. Make sure to visit Graveface Records & Curiosities, a quirky record store that also sells oddities and curiosities - perfect for unique souvenirs.

2.56 Isle of Hope Marina: A Serene Haven: Escape the city buzz and head to the Isle of Hope Marina, a peaceful retreat locals love. Stroll along the docks, watch the boats gently bob on the water, and enjoy breathtaking sunsets over the salt marsh. It's the ideal spot to unwind and connect with the serenity of nature.

2.57 Fragrant Flora at the Fragrance Garden: Tucked within the Botanical Gardens at Forsyth Park is a hidden treasure known as the Fragrance Garden. A haven for the senses, this lesser-known spot is brimming with fragrant flowers and plants. Close your eyes, and let the garden's ambiance transport you to a world of pure bliss.

And Lastly, a New Favorite!

2.58 Plant Riverside District: Welcome to the vibrant and enchanting world of Plant Riverside District, Savannah's newest and most exciting entertainment destination! Nestled along the banks of the Savannah River, this sprawling district is a playground of delights, offering a harmonious blend of history, entertainment, dining, and luxury accommodations.

The History: A Riverside Power Plant Reimagined

Before its transformation into the Plant Riverside District, this 1912-built structure was once the Georgia Power Plant, providing electricity to Savannah for over a century. Today, this historic landmark has been ingeniously repurposed to house an array of experiences that honor its industrial heritage while introducing a new era of entertainment and culture.

The JW Marriott Savannah

The JW Marriott Savannah Plant Riverside District is the crown jewel of this destination, offering luxurious accommodations with unparalleled views of the river and the city's iconic skyline. Embrace Southern hospitality with modern elegance in each guest room, and unwind at the rooftop pool while taking in breathtaking vistas.

Entertainment Extravaganza

The Plant Riverside District is much more than a hotel; it's an all-encompassing entertainment hub. The district's crown jewel, "Electric Moon," is a multi-sensory show that illuminates the night with stunning visuals and immersive experiences, making it a must-see for visitors of all ages.

Dine Like Royalty

Enjoy a delicious and delightful culinary journey at any of the many dining options within Plant Riverside District. From upscale rooftop dining at Peregrin to mouthwatering Southern comfort food at River House Savannah, each restaurant offers a unique dining experience with unparalleled riverfront views.

Shopping Extravaganza

Plant Riverside District is a sanctuary for those who love to shop featuring a variety of shops and speciality retailers. There's something for every shopaholic's taste, from high-end couture to locally crafted souvenirs.

The Spirit of Savannah

Incorporating elements of Savannah's rich heritage, the Plant Riverside District exudes the city's spirit, blending history with modernity and showcasing the vibrant culture that has drawn visitors to this city for generations. So, dear adventurer, whether you're seeking a luxurious stay, a culinary exploration, a night of entertainment, or a walk through enchanting gardens, Plant Riverside District awaits with open arms. Embark on a journey through time and indulgence at this riverside wonderland, where the past meets the present in a symphony of excitement. Embrace the spirit of Savannah and create memories to cherish for a lifetime in this captivating destination right beside the Savannah River.

So there you have it, my friend, a glimpse inside some of Savannah's best-kept secrets. Savannah's hidden treasures await individuals with an inquisitive spirit and a taste for the unexpected. From secret gardens and artsy alleyways to haunted legends and culinary delights, these hidden jewels are just waiting for the adventurous traveler in you to discover them. So take a detour, embrace the unknown, and let Savannah's mysteries unveil themselves in all their splendor! Happy exploring, and may Savannah's secret treasures capture your heart!

Chapter 3

You Have a Lot of Options In How, Or Where, You Explore Savannah

Other than driving about, there are various convenient and entertaining methods to see Savannah's remarkably diversified sights and attractions. Let's take a few moments to discover the many lovely ways Savannah welcomes you to explore its iconic sites and hidden jewels.

3.1. Trolley Tours: Step aboard one of Savannah's iconic trolleys and prepare to be whisked away on a captivating journey through time. These charming trolley tours offer the perfect blend of entertainment and education, making them an ideal choice for history buffs and curious explorers alike.

As you roll along the city's picturesque streets, your friendly guide will entertain you with tales about Savannah's captivating past, sharing stories of famous figures, historical events, and even a few local legends. Whether you're a first-time visitor or a seasoned Savannah enthusiast, these trolley tours promise an enchanting ride through the heart and soul of this beautiful city.

3.2. Walking Tours: For those who prefer to savor every nuance of Savannah's enchanting atmosphere, lace up your walking shoes and prepare for a delightful stroll through history. Exploring the Historic District on foot is like stepping into a living time capsule.

As you wander through the meticulously manicured squares and beneath ancient oak canopies, you'll feel a profound connection to the city's past. Expert guides will share fascinating insights into Savannah's unique architecture, hidden alleys, and quirky anecdotes you might never discover. From the hallowed grounds of historic homes to the charming secrets tucked away in every corner, walking tours promise an intimate and immersive experience of Savannah's soulful charm.

3.3. Horse-Drawn Carriages: In the mood for a touch of old-world romance? Climb aboard one of Savannah's iconic horse-drawn carriages and let the rhythmic clip-clop of hooves transport you back to a bygone era. With each gentle sway of the carriage, you'll find yourself immersed in the romance and elegance of the city's historic allure.

Expertly narrated by experienced carriage drivers, these tours take you on a leisurely journey through Savannah's enchanting squares and past stately mansions adorned with intricate ironwork. As the city's captivating tales unfold before you, you can't help but feel a sense of timeless magic in the air.

3.4. Bicycle Rentals: Seeking a more active and adventurous way to explore the city? Look no further than renting a bicycle. Pedal your way through Savannah's charming streets and picturesque neighborhoods, where each turn reveals a new treasure waiting to be discovered.

With the freedom to chart your own course, you can meander through the Historic District, dip into vibrant art galleries, and find hidden parks that offer a break from the hustle and bustle. Besides being an eco-friendly choice, bicycle rentals provide a refreshing breeze and a chance to work off some of those delectable Savannah treats you will surely enjoy along the way!

3.5. Scooter Rentals: Ready to zip around Savannah with a dash of flair? Scooter rentals offer a fun and zippy way to navigate the city's charming streets. You'll experience a unique sense of freedom and excitement as you whiz by historic landmarks and delightful squares. Whether cruising along the waterfront or heading to a favorite eatery, scooters are a convenient mode of transportation and an excellent opportunity to immerse yourself in Savannah's vibrant atmosphere.

3.6. Riverboat Cruises: Take your Savannah adventure to the water and set sail on a riverboat cruise along the majestic Savannah River. With the breeze in your hair and the sun on your face, you'll be treated to breathtaking views of the city's skyline and iconic landmarks.

As you glide along the river, you'll gain a new perspective on Savannah's rich history and enduring relationship with the river. Riverboat trips promise a fascinating and wonderful experience, whether it's a leisurely midday cruise or a romantic evening underneath the stars.

3.7. Segway Tours: Embrace modern technology and channel your inner explorer by taking a Segway tour. Glide through Savannah's streets easily and cover more ground than you would on foot. With some practice, you'll be effortlessly zipping through the city, enjoying the sights and sounds of Savannah's vibrant districts. Guided by knowledgeable locals, Segway tours offer a dynamic way to discover various attractions while adding excitement to your journey.

3.8. Public Transportation: Budget-conscious travelers, rejoice! Savannah offers public transportation options, including buses and shuttles, making it easy to hop on and off at various landmarks. As you ride alongside friendly locals, you'll get a sense of the city's vibrant pulse and immerse yourself in the local culture. It's an excellent way to explore Savannah while tasting authentic Savannah life.

3.9. Sip and Shop Tours: Indulge in a delightful combination of retail therapy and libations on a Sip and Shop tour. Explore Savannah's charming boutiques, art galleries, and unique stores while savoring local wines or craft beers. Whether hunting for souvenirs or updating your wardrobe with Savannah style, these tours offer a fun and relaxed way to discover the city's shopping scene.

3.10. Ghost Tours: Prepare to be spooked as you venture into the haunted history of Savannah on a ghost tour. As the sun sets, the city's streets come alive with eerie tales of restless spirits and haunted buildings. Walk through dimly lit alleyways and shadowy squares, and listen to chilling stories of Savannah's ghostly residents. For those who crave a taste of the supernatural, a ghost tour is an unforgettable adventure into the mysterious side of the city.

3.11. Golf Cart Tours: For a breezy and entertaining way to explore Savannah, hop on a golf cart tour. Zip through the city's picturesque streets and uncover its architectural treasures, historic sites, and beautiful parks. Expert guides will lead the way, sharing fascinating stories and trivia, making this a comfortable and informative journey for all.

3.12. Food Tours: Calling all foodies! Embark on a mouthwatering adventure through Savannah's culinary delights on a food tour. Sample the city's most delectable dishes, from Southern classics to innovative gastronomic creations. As you savor each tasty bite, you'll also learn about the rich food culture that has shaped Savannah's culinary scene over the years.

3.13. Architectural Tours: Immerse yourself in the diverse architectural wonders that grace Savannah's streets on an architectural tour. From elegant antebellum mansions to striking Gothic Revival churches, Savannah boasts an array of architectural styles that narrate the city's vibrant past. As you stroll through the city's neighborhoods, you'll gain a deeper appreciation for the craftsmanship and artistry that define Savannah's unique character.

3.14. Drag Queen-Guided Pub Crawl: For a fabulous and entertaining night out, join a drag queen-guided pub crawl in Savannah! Experience the city's vibrant nightlife like never before as glamorous drag queens lead you to the hottest bars and liveliest venues in town. Prepare for a night of laughter, dancing, and unforgettable performances, all while exploring Savannah's vibrant bar scene. These tours are not only a celebration of LGBTQ+ culture but also a fantastic way to meet new people, make memories, and dance the night away in true Savannah style!

3.15. Tybee Island Dolphin Cruise: Escape to the scenic shores of Tybee Island for an enchanting dolphin cruise. Hop aboard a boat and set sail in search of playful dolphins frolicking in the pristine waters of the Atlantic Ocean. As you cruise along the coast, you'll also soak in breathtaking views of Tybee's sandy beaches and picturesque landscapes. This family-friendly excursion offers a chance to connect with nature and witness these graceful marine creatures in their natural habitat, creating memories that will linger long after you return to the mainland.

3.16. Pedal Power - Bike Tours: Get those legs moving and pedal through Savannah's picturesque streets on a bike tour! Feel the breeze in your hair as you leisurely cycle past the historic squares, charming architecture, and lush parks. It's more than just a fun and eco-friendly way to explore. Still, it also allows you to stop and snap Insta-worthy photos whenever inspiration strikes!

3.17. Water Adventures - Kayaking and Paddleboarding: Savannah's rivers call! Take a kayak or paddleboard out for a ride around the marshes and rivers. Float through unspoiled spaces and wildlife while taking in the tranquil beauty of the South. It's an immersive experience that takes you into Savannah's breathtaking scenery and allows you to connect with nature in a whole new way.

3.18. Funky Pedicab Tours: Ready for a whimsical adventure? Hop aboard a funky pedicab and let your "bike chauffeur" take you on a thrilling ride through the city's vibrant neighborhoods. It's a quirky and fun way to explore, with your guide adding a dash of humor and local flavor to the mix as you cruise in style!

3.19. Scenic Riverwalk Strolls: Lace up those walking shoes and stroll along Savannah's famous Riverwalk. This bustling promenade hugs the Savannah River, offering stunning views of the waterfront, historic landmarks, and bustling River Street. It's the perfect spot to people-watch, snap photos, and soak in the lively ambiance.

Now, my fellow adventurers, with all these delightful ways to explore Savannah's enchanting landmarks, you're all set to enjoy a journey filled with history, charm, and the warm embrace of this lovely city. Whichever mode of exploration you choose, you're in for an unforgettable adventure that will leave you with cherished memories of your time in the heart of the South.

Whether you're gliding on a Segway, wandering through haunted alleys, savoring the city's flavors, or setting sail on the river, each adventure promises to leave you with lasting memories and a newfound love for the enchanting city of Savannah. So, dive in, sip and shop, uncover ghostly tales, and revel in the charm and culture of this delightful Southern gem – Savannah awaits your discovery!

Chapter 4

Local Favorites - Hidden Gems in Savannah, GA

Hey there, fellow adventurers! Get ready to explore Savannah like an authentic native as we discover some hidden jewels and local favorites that are only rarely on the radar of visitors.

In this chapter, we'll take you off the beaten path to discover the quirky, charming, and lesser-known spots that the locals hold near and dear to their hearts. Alright, let's spill the beans on some local secrets! If you really want to experience Savannah like a true insider, you've got to check out these incredible places.

Step one, start your day with a coffee fix at The Sentient Bean, where they serve up more than just your usual brew – it's a whole vibe! And speaking of vibes, you can't miss Starland Yard – an outdoor food truck park with live music and flavors from around the world. It's the perfect spot for a laid-back evening.

Oh, and if you're a collector of rare books and old collectibles like me, Alex Raskin Antiques is a must-see. You might stumble upon a literary gem from the past!

Alright, my friends, are you ready to uncover the true heart and soul of Savannah? Let's dive into the adventures and create memories that'll last a lifetime! So, let's roll up our sleeves and uncover Savannah's best-kept secrets together! Let's go exploring!

4.1 Leopold's Ice Cream (212 E Broughton St, Savannah, GA 31401): First stop, the sweetest spot in town – Leopold's Ice Cream! Established in 1919, this vintage ice cream parlor is a must-visit for anyone with a sweet tooth. Get ready to indulge in classic flavors like Tutti Frutti and Butter Pecan, served in old-fashioned soda fountain style. The charming décor and friendly staff make this place feel like a time capsule, taking you back to the golden age of ice cream parlors. Don't miss out on their signature "Savannah Socialite" sundae – a heavenly concoction that'll leave you floating on a cloud of sugar-induced bliss!

4.2 Back in the Day Bakery (2403 Bull St, Savannah, GA 31401): Are you ready to be transported to pastry heaven? Look no further than Back in the Day Bakery. With its delightful aroma of freshly baked goodies, this cozy little bakery will capture your heart from the moment you step in.

Everything here is made with love and local ingredients, from buttery biscuits and flaky croissants to the most divine cupcakes and pies you'll ever eat. You might even spot locals gathered over a cup of coffee, cherishing the simple joy of great company and even better desserts.

Tip: Try their famous "Old-Fashioned Chocolate Pie" – a slice of velvety chocolate heaven that will have you daydreaming about it for days!

4.3 Wormsloe Historic Site (7601 Skidaway Rd, Savannah, GA 31406): Alright, history buffs, this one's for you! Escape the city's hustle and bustle and venture into the enchanting beauty of the Wormsloe Historic Site. As you drive down the awe-inspiring avenue lined with majestic live oak trees dripping with Spanish moss, you'll feel like you've stepped into a fairytale.

The ruins of this colonial estate and the lush surroundings create a magical ambiance, making it the perfect spot for a leisurely stroll or a picturesque photo op. It's no surprise that people go here for some soul-soothing solitude and a reflection of the historic past that shaped their beloved Savannah.

4.4 Bluff Drive (Isle of Hope, Savannah, GA 31406): Want to experience the picturesque charm of Savannah's riverside neighborhoods? Look no further than Bluff Drive on the Isle of Hope. This scenic drive offers breathtaking views of the Intracoastal Waterway, with elegant historic homes and lush gardens adding to the visual feast. Locals adore taking leisurely drives along this picturesque route, savoring the beauty of the Spanish moss-draped oaks and the refreshing river breeze. With every turn of the road, you'll feel like you're stepping into a postcard-worthy scene.

4.5 The Grey (109 Martin Luther King Jr Blvd, Savannah, GA 31401): When dining in Savannah, The Grey is a standout gem that locals can't get enough of. Set in a restored Greyhound bus terminal, this stylish restaurant offers an exquisite fusion of Southern cuisine and international flavors.

The elegant and modern ambiance, combined with the warm hospitality of the staff, creates a dining experience that is both refined and approachable. The ever-changing menu highlights the best local and seasonal ingredients, resulting in dishes that are as artful as they are delicious. A meal at The Grey is a true gastronomic journey that will leave you with a newfound appreciation for Savannah's culinary scene.

4.6 Forsyth Farmers' Market (13 E Park Ave, Savannah, GA 31401): Head over to the Forsyth Farmers' Market for an authentic taste of Savannah's local produce and vibrant community spirit. Held every Saturday in the city's heart, this bustling market offers a cornucopia of fresh fruits, vegetables, artisanal products, and delectable treats from local vendors.

Join the locals as they meander through the colorful stalls, chatting with farmers and artisans and sampling the freshest produce. It's the perfect opportunity to connect with the heart and soul of Savannah's local food scene while supporting the hardworking farmers and producers who make it all possible.

4.7 The Sentient Bean (13 E Park Ave, Savannah, GA 31401): Coffee lovers, this one's for you! The Sentient Bean is a beloved local hangout, serving up some of the best coffee in town with a side of artsy charm. This bohemian café is a hub for artists, students, and creative minds, making it the perfect spot to soak in Savannah's eclectic vibe. The cozy atmosphere and welcoming staff make it a favorite place to linger with a book, catch up with friends, or people-watch from the sidewalk patio. Whether you prefer a classic cappuccino or a specialty vegan latte, The Sentient Bean has something special for all your caffeine cravings!

4.8 Skidaway Island State Park (52 Diamond Causeway, Savannah, GA 31411): Nature enthusiasts, rejoice! Skidaway Island State Park is a local treasure that offers a perfect escape into the great outdoors. Lace up your hiking boots and hit the trails as you explore the park's diverse ecosystems, including marshes, forests, and tidal creeks.

Don't forget your binoculars – the park is a haven for birdwatchers, with countless species to spot along the way. Locals often come here for peaceful walks, picnics under the moss-draped oaks, and a chance to reconnect with nature's beauty, just a stone's throw away from the city's lively atmosphere.

4.9 Vic's on the River (26 E Bay St, Savannah, GA 31401): Ready for a dining experience that combines Southern elegance with breathtaking river views? Vic's on the River has got you covered! Housed in a historic cotton warehouse overlooking the Savannah River, this elegant restaurant blends classic Southern dishes and modern culinary twists.

The upscale ambiance, with its charming balcony and attentive service, makes it a favorite spot for special occasions and romantic evenings. Watching the boats sail by as the sun sets over the river is a moment that will stay etched in your memory forever. Be sure to try their famous "Shrimp & Grits" – a beloved Southern classic with a touch of Vic's culinary magic!

4.10 Sandfly BBQ (8413 Ferguson Ave, Savannah, GA 31406): Regarding finger-licking barbecue, locals know that Sandfly BBQ is the place to go. Tucked away in the charming Sandfly neighborhood, this unassuming spot is a haven for barbecue enthusiasts. The mouthwatering aroma of smoked meats will draw you in, and the juicy, flavorful ribs, pulled pork, and brisket will keep you coming back for more.

Try their tangy, house-made barbecue sauces that elevate the flavors to a whole new level. With communal picnic tables and a laid-back vibe, Sandfly BBQ is the perfect place to roll up your sleeves and dig into a true Southern barbecue feast.

4.11 The Coffee Fox (102 W Broughton St, Savannah, GA 31401): Calling all coffee connoisseurs and caffeine aficionados! The Coffee Fox is a charming specialty coffee shop in downtown Savannah's heart. With a passion for exceptional coffee and a cozy, artsy ambiance, this local favorite serves various expertly crafted espresso drinks, pour-overs, and cold brews.

Their skilled baristas take pride in sourcing the finest coffee beans and carefully preparing each cup. Pair your brew with one of their delectable pastries or cookies for the ultimate indulgence. Grab your coffee to-go and explore the city's historic streets, or cozy up in the shop and soak in Savannah's vibrant atmosphere.

4.12 Tybee Island Dolphin Cruise: A visit to Savannah wouldn't be complete without a tour of Tybee Island and a thrilling dolphin cruise. Set sail from Lazaretto Creek on a trip of marine exploration. Make sure to keep a watch out for playful dolphins as they cruise effortlessly alongside the boat. Make sure your camera is ready to record these beautiful moments. The seasoned crew will give fascinating insights on the regional wildlife and ecosystem, making this an interesting and unforgettable experience for people of all ages. This trip is an excellent addition to any Savannah adventure.

4.13 Local Breweries and Brewpubs: When the sun sets over Savannah, locals head to the city's fantastic breweries and brew pubs to taste the region's craft beer scene. From Southbound Brewing Co. to Service Brewing Co., these local breweries offer a diverse array of craft beers, from refreshing IPAs to rich stouts. Many of these establishments also host live music and food trucks, creating a lively and sociable atmosphere perfect for mingling with the friendly locals. So, grab a cold pint, make new friends, and savor the unique flavors of Savannah's craft brews as you soak in the city's vibrant nightlife.

4.14 Blue Orb Ghost Tours (1 E Broughton St, Savannah, GA 31401): Brace yourself for a spine-tingling adventure as we dive into Savannah's haunted history with Blue Orb Ghost Tours. Led by expert storytellers and paranormal enthusiasts, these walking tours take you through the city's most haunted locations. Listen to chilling tales of ghostly apparitions, unsolved mysteries, and eerie encounters that will send shivers down your spine. Whether you're a skeptic or a believer in the supernatural, these ghost tours offer a fascinating glimpse into the darker side of Savannah's past and the lingering spirits that call this city home.

4.15 Grayson Stadium (1401 E Victory Dr, Savannah, GA 31404): Calling all sports fans! A trip to Savannah would be incomplete without attending a baseball game at Grayson Stadium. This historic stadium, which is home to the Savannah Bananas, a collegiate summer league baseball team, provides a fun and exciting atmosphere for sports fans of all ages. Join the locals in cheering on their favorite team, savoring the vibrant ballpark entertainment, and relishing traditional ballpark specialties like hot dogs and peanuts. It's a classic American experience that will leave you in Savannah with memories of cheering, laughter, and the joy of community.

4.16 Little Duck Diner (150 W Saint Julian St, Savannah, GA 31401): If you're craving a quirky dining experience with a retro twist, look no further than Little Duck Diner. This vibrant and playful eatery serves up classic diner fare with a modern flair, all set in a whimsical, art-deco-inspired ambiance. From mouthwatering burgers and indulgent milkshakes to inventive dishes like lobster corn dogs, the menu is a delightful fusion of comfort food and gourmet creations. The bright colors, funky decor, and friendly service create an atmosphere as fun as the delicious food, making Little Duck Diner a hit with locals and visitors alike.

4.17 Daffin Park (1301 E Victory Dr, Savannah, GA 31404): It's time to get away from the city and reconnect with nature at Daffin Park, a preferred local green retreat. This vast park has plenty of space for picnics, leisurely walks, and family-friendly activities. Play frisbee in the wide fields, enjoy a relaxing stroll around the lake, or challenge your friends to a tennis match on the courts. Daffin Park is great for a relaxing day outdoors in Savannah, with shaded walks, a play area for kids, and plenty of green space to rest.

4.18 The Book Lady Bookstore (6 E Liberty St, Savannah, GA 31401): This amazing compact bookstore is a must-see for book lovers and literature fans. The Book Lady Bookstore is a unique treasure chest of new and secondhand books in a variety of categories. The warm and inviting atmosphere is ideal for getting lost in a good book or discovering your next literary find. The helpful staff is always willing to make suggestions and engage in book-related discussions. So go ahead and look around, immerse yourself in a world of words, and come out with a new favorite read!

4.19 Lafayette Square Fountain: Discover a hidden gem in Lafayette Square – a tranquil fountain that locals adore. This beautiful spot is a favorite among Savannahians for peaceful reflection and relaxation. Tucked away in the heart of the Historic District, the fountain's gentle murmur and the lush greenery create a soothing ambiance that provides respite from the bustling city life. Take a seat on a nearby bench, feel the cool mist on your face, and enjoy the blissful tranquility of the Lafayette Square Fountain.

4.20 Savannah Bee Company (104 W Broughton St, Savannah, GA 31401): If you're looking for a unique souvenir to take home from your Savannah adventure, head over to the Savannah Bee Company. This charming store is a haven for honey enthusiasts, offering a delightful array of premium honey products. From luscious honeycomb chunks to artisanal honey spreads, you'll find a variety of delectable treats to satisfy your sweet cravings.

Take advantage of their specialty honey varieties like Tupelo and Sourwood, known for their exceptional flavors. Plus, you can sample different types of honey to find your favorite before purchasing. It's a bee-utiful way to support local beekeepers and bring a taste of Savannah's sweetness back with you.

4.21 Smith Brothers Butcher Shop (535 E Liberty St, Savannah, GA 31401): This one's for you, carnivores! Step inside Smith Brothers Butcher Shop, an esteemed neighborhood institution where quality and skill reign supreme. With a focus on getting high-quality, locally farmed meats, this family-owned butcher shop is a favorite among foodies and chefs. Smith Brothers' skilled butchers can certainly assist you in choosing the ideal meat for your gourmet pursuits, whether you're looking for the perfect cut of steak, pork chops, or juicy sausages. Aside from their great meats, they offer artisanal cheeses, house-made marinades, and premium ingredients to boost your home cooking to restaurant-quality heights.

4.22 The Foundery Coffee Pub (1313 Habersham St, Savannah, GA 31401): You're invited to the Foundery Coffee Pub, a lovely coffeehouse/community hub hybrid. This unique cafe is a favorite gathering place for Savannah natives, offering an inviting space where you can sip expertly made coffee while having conversations with friends or simply spending some time by yourself.

The Foundery prides itself on fostering a sense of community, and you'll often find local artists showcasing their work or community events taking place here. Don't miss their signature "Savannah Fog" – a unique twist on a London Fog that combines earl grey tea, steamed milk, and a dash of honey. It's the perfect sip for a laid-back afternoon in Savannah.

4.23 Little Gracie Statue in Bonaventure Cemetery: A little-known beauty contains a touching and tragic story. The Little Gracie Statue, located in Bonaventure Cemetery, is a memorial to Gracie Watson, a young girl who died unexpectedly at the age of six. The acclaimed sculptor John Walz made the statue, which captures Gracie's likeness with eerily lifelike detail, making it a painful and compelling sight. Locals frequently visit this statue, giving tokens of affection as a tribute to the memory of a small girl who snatched the hearts of everyone who heard her story.

4.24 Sentient Bean Community Stage (13 East Park Avenue, Savannah, GA, 31401): Not only does The Sentient Bean (mentioned earlier) boast fantastic coffee, but it also features a hidden gem for local artists and performers – the Sentient Bean Community Stage. This cozy spot regularly hosts live music performances, poetry readings, open mic nights, and other artistic events. Locals flock to this stage to showcase their talents, listen to live music, and support their fellow creatives. If you visit during one of these events, you'll see Savannah's vibrant arts scene and experience the city's creative spirit.

4.25 Tybee Island Social Club (1311 Butler Ave, Tybee Island, GA 31328): Let's venture back to Tybee Island for a taste of the island's quirky charm at the Tybee Island Social Club. This beloved local hangout serves up a fusion of Caribbean and Southern flavors, creating an exciting and comforting culinary experience. The laid-back atmosphere and friendly staff make it a go-to spot for locals seeking a taste of the island's eclectic vibe. Whether you're craving a mouthwatering jerk chicken sandwich or their famous "Bangin' Shrimp & Grits," the Tybee Island Social Club will surely delight your taste buds and leave you with a smile.

4.26 Tiedeman Park (Savannah, GA 31406): When Savannahians seek a peaceful retreat from the city's bustling streets, they head to Tiedeman Park. This hidden oasis is a local favorite for picnics, yoga sessions, and unwinding amidst nature's embrace. Stroll through the shady trails, breathe in the fresh air, and enjoy the serenity of this secret spot.

Tiedeman Park is the perfect escape for a quiet moment of reflection or a leisurely afternoon with friends and family. Whether you're picnicking under the oak trees or simply taking in the beauty of the landscape, here you'll find a sense of tranquility that embodies Savannah's slower pace of life.

You'll discover the heart and soul of this wonderful city as you wander off the beaten path and explore Savannah's local favorites. These lesser-known treasures showcase the city's original charm and the warmth of its friendly residents, from hidden eateries and small coffee shops to quiet parks and touching memorials. So, take your time exploring these unique locations and submerge yourself in the culture like a local - these are just a few of the many things that make Savannah a genuinely exceptional destination. Have fun exploring!

Chapter 5

Adventure Out Onto Savannah's Islands

Welcome to island life, fellow adventurers! As we leave Savannah's crowded downtown, we are lured into the tranquil charms of its adjacent islands. Nature and seaside beauty coexist in this peaceful haven. This chapter will take us to the sandy beaches of Tybee Island and the lovely trails of Skidaway Island State Park.

There are a couple more islands near Savannah that provide unique experiences and exploration possibilities. Let's take a look at a selection of these enthralling islands. So grab your sun hat, apply some sunscreen, and prepare to have some island fun. Expect to be wowed by sandy beaches, coastline views, and wildlife encounters that will have you feel like you've stepped into a tropical paradise.

5.1 Tybee Island: Tybee Island, just a short drive from Savannah's Historic District, tempts with its laid-back atmosphere and sandy coastline. Pack your beach bag, reapply that sunscreen, and prepare to enjoy the sun on Tybee's lovely beaches. Tybee has something for everyone, whether you're a beach bum trying to relax or a water sports junkie eager to ride the waves. The island's fluid atmosphere is contagious; locals and visitors alike can be found enjoying the surf, sampling seafood delicacies, and checking out the historic Tybee Island Lighthouse.

5.2 Tybee Island Lighthouse (30 Meddin Dr, Tybee Island, GA 31328): A visit to Tybee Island wouldn't be complete without climbing to the top of the Tybee Island Lighthouse. This historical site provides expansive shoreline views, making it the perfect spot for a photo-worthy moment. As you climb the 178 steps to the top, you might hear fascinating stories about the lighthouse's maritime history. From the sea breezes to the captivating vistas, the Tybee Island Lighthouse experience is a quintessential island adventure you won't want to miss.

5.3 Skidaway Island State Park (52 Diamond Causeway, Savannah, GA 31411): Nature enthusiasts, welcome! Skidaway Island State Park is an unspoiled treasure just a short drive from the bustling streets of Savannah. This coastal paradise offers a wonderful escape into nature's arms with its network of nature paths, salt marshes, and tidal streams. Put on your hiking boots and explore the park's magnificent walkways, where you might come across animals such as deer, fiddler crabs, and a variety of bird species. Don't forget to bring your camera; the views of the salt marsh are simply spectacular. Skidaway Island State Park delivers a memorable day of adventure and natural beauty, whether you're a seasoned hiker or a leisurely jogger.

5.4 Wassaw Island: Wassaw Island, located just off the coast of Savannah, is a pristine and untamed barrier island that has mostly avoided interference from humans. The island provides a protected habitat for a variety of wildlife, including nesting sea turtles, migratory birds, and numerous marine species, as part of the Wassaw National Wildlife Refuge. Wassaw Island, accessible only by boat, provides tourists with a rare opportunity to appreciate the grandeur of unspoiled nature. Hiking trails weave through marine woods and along the sandy shoreline, revealing the island's natural wonders. Birdwatchers will be delighted by the richness of bird life.

5.5 Little Tybee Island: Little Tybee Island, positioned adjacent to Tybee Island, provides a more isolated and off-the-beaten-path experience. The island is only accessible by boat or kayak and is uninhabited and untamed, providing a sense of unspoiled escape. Little Tybee Island is a nature lover's paradise, with huge marshes, tidal rivers, and pristine shores. Visitors can explore the island's different ecosystems, keep an eye out for playful dolphins in the surrounding waters, and witness the enchantment of bioluminescence on particular nights when the water shines with a beautiful blue light. Guided boat cruises and kayak adventures are popular methods to discover Little Tybee Island's hidden gems.

5.6 Cockspur Island: Situated near the entrance to the Savannah River, Cockspur Island is home to the historic Cockspur Island Lighthouse. While smaller than Tybee Island, this lesser-known island holds great historical significance. The lighthouse, constructed in the 1850s, was vital in guiding ships into the busy port of Savannah. Guests can discover the island's history and the lighthouse's important role at the nearby visitor center. In addition to the lighthouse, Cockspur Island also offers picnic areas and scenic spots along the river, making it a fun destination for a relaxing day trip.

5.7 Lazaretto Creek: Encounter Dolphins and More! Lazaretto Creek is not only just a beautiful waterway; it is also an ideal starting point for remarkable outings. Explore the marshes by boat, spot playful dolphins, and visit the lovely Cockspur Island and its lighthouse. This creek is popular among locals looking for an authentic coastal experience due to its calm waters and an abundance of wildlife.

5.8 Oatland Island Wildlife Center (711 Sandtown Rd, Savannah, GA 31410): Oatland Island Wildlife Center is a great place to get up close and personal with wildlife. Many different creatures such as bison, bobcats, and gray wolves call this hidden oasis home. Stroll along the boardwalks and immerse yourself inside these fascinating creatures' natural surroundings. It's a fun family activity that will leave you with cherished memories.

The islands located near Savannah provide unique visitor experiences and an opportunity to connect with nature in its most basic form. Each island has its own charm, from pristine beaches to unspoiled landscapes, inviting visitors to leave the frantic pace of the city and experience the peace of the coastal wildness. Suppose you're looking for a more remote and quiet adventure during your visit to Savannah. In such cases, these nearby islands are ideal for experiencing the beauty of nature and creating amazing memories.

So get in your car, roll down your windows, and follow the salty sea breezes to Tybee Island and Skidaway Island State Park. These island retreats will add a touch of beauty to your Savannah journey, from sandy toes to peaceful pathways. Make your arrangements now to have a unique experience while visiting Savannah's island jewels! These tropical beauties will not disappoint.

Chapter 6

Exciting Sporting Events in Savannah, GA

Participating in or watching one of these local athletic events is a fun and exciting way to immerse yourself in Savannah's lively community spirit. Whether you're rooting for baseball players, jogging over bridges, swinging golf clubs, or experiencing the excitement of hockey games, these athletic activities add an exciting component to your Savannah holiday.

Savannah's athletic competitions are more than just a chance to cheer for your favorite team; they are a vital part of the city's dynamic culture and sense of camaraderie. So let's take a look at some of the local favorites, and the hidden gems of Savannah's sporting culture, and see where the thrill of the game connects with Southern hospitality!

Here are a few you should check out for yourself the next time you're in Savannah.

6.1 Savannah Bananas: Grayson Stadium, 1401 E Victory Dr, Savannah, GA 31404: Step into the lively world of baseball with the Savannah Bananas! Grayson Stadium, home to the Savannah Bananas, is the place to be for an unforgettable baseball experience. Known for their entertaining antics, the Bananas deliver a unique and family-friendly atmosphere that goes beyond the game. From dance-offs and mascot shenanigans to engaging the audience in wild cheers and activities between innings, the Bananas bring a whole new level of excitement to the sport. Join the rowdy crowd, don your Banana-themed gear, and get ready to root for Savannah's beloved baseball team!

6.2 Rock 'n' Roll Marathon: Lace up your running shoes and hit the streets of Savannah during the annual Rock 'n' Roll Marathon! This electrifying event combines the thrill of running with the beats of live music. The marathon route takes you through Savannah's scenic and historic neighborhoods, allowing you to absorb the city's beauty while keeping your spirits high, with live bands and DJs performing along the course. Whether you're a seasoned runner looking for a new challenge or a first-timer seeking a fun and engaging race, the Rock 'n' Roll Marathon is a fantastic way to experience Savannah from a different perspective. The starting location for the Rock 'n' Roll Marathon may vary each year, so be sure to check the official event website for updated information.

6.3 Savannah Golf Championship (25 Deer Creek Dr, Savannah, GA 31411): Calling all golf enthusiasts! The Savannah Golf Championship is a local favorite sporting event that showcases professional golfers competing at the Deer Creek Course in The Landings Club. This PGA TOUR-sanctioned event brings in players from all across the world, providing an excellent opportunity to witness top-tier golfing talent in action. The stunning coastal setting and challenging course make for an exciting and memorable golfing experience.

6.4 Savannah Bridge Run: If you're a fan of running and exploring Savannah's scenic beauty, the Savannah Bridge Run is an event not to be missed. The yearly competition involves crossing the Talmadge Memorial Bridge for competitors, offering breathtaking views of the Savannah River and the city skyline. Runners can choose between various distances, from a 5K to a 15K race, catering to all skill levels. It's a fantastic opportunity to embrace Savannah's active community and be part of a vibrant running event. The Savannah Bridge Run's opening location changes each year, so be sure to visit the official event website for the most up-to-date information.

6.5 Savannah Hockey Classic: The annual Savannah Hockey Classic, held at the Savannah Civic Center, is sure to thrill ice hockey lovers. Teams from the University of Georgia, Georgia Tech, Florida, and Florida State University compete in this invitational collegiate hockey event. The raucous audiences and rapid-fire activity on the ice create an exciting atmosphere that draws sports fans from all over the region.

So, my sporty friend, there you have it - just a few of Savannah's hidden gems in the sporting world! From the Savannah Bananas' entertaining baseball games to the Rock 'n' Roll Marathon's music-filled running adventure, these local favorites offer a unique and immersive experience of Savannah's sporting culture. Join the locals in celebrating the spirit of competition and revel in the joy of being a part of something special. Happy cheering, and may your Savannah sporting escapades be filled with fun and memorable moments!

Chapter 7

Wildlife Encounters and Animal Excursions

Greetings from Savannah's wild side! In this chapter, we'll take you on thrilling wildlife encounters and animal adventures that will get you up close and personal with the fascinating animals that live in this region. These interactions will leave you with precious memories that will last a lifetime, whether you are an environmentalist, an animal fanatic, or just curious about the rich species that flourish in and around Savannah.

A natural wonderland awaits you within the heart of Savannah. These wildlife experiences and animal tours promise a really memorable experience, from experiencing native species in their original surroundings to seeing playful dolphins out in the open water to examining the underwater world of Skidaway Island's aquarium.

7.1 Oatland Island Wildlife Center (711 Sandtown Rd, Savannah, GA 31410): Are you ready to meet some of Georgia's most captivating native animals? Look no further than the Oatland Island Wildlife Center, a hidden gem in a lush coastal landscape. This wildlife haven offers a natural habitat setting where you can observe and interact with various animals, each playing a vital role in the region's delicate ecosystem. Walk along the meandering trails as curious bobcats peer from their enclosures, or catch a glimpse of the elusive wolves roaming freely in spacious habitats. The Oatland Island Wildlife Center is more than just a zoo; it's an educational hub where you can learn about wildlife conservation and the importance of preserving these magnificent creatures. Ideal for families and solo travelers alike.

7.2 Dolphin-Watching Tours: Get ready for an aquatic adventure like no other as we set sail on a dolphin-watching tour! Savannah's coastal waters are teeming with the joyful playmates of the sea: the Atlantic bottlenose dolphins. These intelligent and social creatures love to show off their acrobatic skills, leaping and gliding alongside boats in a mesmerizing dance. As you embark on a dolphin-watching tour, keep your camera ready and your eyes peeled for these charming beings. Feel the thrill of the open water and the gentle breeze on your face as you cruise along the Savannah River and the estuaries nearby. Numerous tour operators offer these delightful boat excursions, making finding a tour that fits your schedule and budget easy.

7.3 UGA Aquarium on Skidaway Island (30 Ocean Science Circle, Savannah, GA 31411): Dive into the depths of Georgia's marine wonders at the UGA Aquarium on Skidaway Island. Part of the University of Georgia's Marine Extension and Georgia Sea Grant, this facility offers a window into the mysterious underwater world of coastal ecosystems. Explore captivating exhibits that showcase native marine life, from vibrant fish and cute turtles to mesmerizing jellyfish. Educational programs and talks by marine scientists add a layer of insight to your visit, leaving you with a newfound appreciation for the ocean's wonders.

7.4 Tybee Island Sea Life Walking Tours (37 Meddin Drive, Tybee Island, Georgia 31328): Tybee Island is well-known for more than just its white sand beaches; it's also home to an abundance of fascinating marine life. Embark on a sea life walking tour and uncover the secrets of Tybee's coastal habitats with the guidance of expert naturalists. During low tide, the shoreline reveals diverse marine creatures, including sand dollars, starfish, and crabs. These guided walking tours provide an eco-friendly and eye-opening experience suitable for all ages. To join a Tybee Island Sea Life Walking Tour, check with local tour operators or the Tybee Island Visitor Center for availability and departure locations.

Did You Know? Savannah's animal events are not just your typical pet shows; they are heartwarming experiences celebrating the special bond between humans and animals? Let's explore the local favorites and a few of the hidden gems of Savannah's animal world, where furry friends take center stage and create cherished memories!

Here are a few to check out:

7.5 Woof Gang Bakery Doggie Carnival: Calling all dog lovers! The Woof Gang Bakery Doggie Carnival is a tail-wagging extravaganza that brings together pups and their humans for a day of fun and festivities. From playful competitions to doggie treat tasting, this event is a pupper's paradise! Watch furry pals show off their tricks, enjoy pet-friendly vendors, and let your four-legged friend make new buddies. It's a heartwarming celebration of all things canine, Savannah-style!

7.6 Wag-O-Ween Halloween Fun for Furry Companions: Get ready for a howling good time at Wag-O-Ween, Savannah's most adorable pet costume party! Held around Halloween, this furry fiesta invites pets and their owners to dress in creative and cute costumes. Be amazed by the sheer creativity as pups and even some brave felines strut their stuff. The event also hosts a pet parade, where each adorable participant gets their moment in the spotlight. It's a picture-perfect opportunity to capture your furry friend's Halloween spirit!

7.7 Tails & Ales: Savannah knows how to combine two great loves - dogs and craft beer! Tails & Ales is a unique event that pairs local craft breweries with doggie-friendly activities. Sip on your favorite brews while your furry buddy enjoys playtime with other pups in the beer garden. The event supports local animal shelters and rescue organizations, so you can raise a toast to a good cause while bonding with fellow pet lovers.

7.8 Pet Picnics at Forsyth Park: Picture this: A lovely day at Forsyth Park, surrounded by beautiful scenery and joyful dogs, and the aroma of delicious cookouts in the air. Join the locals and their four-legged friends for a fun pet picnic! Spread out a blanket, prepare a good meal, and let your pet enjoy an outdoor getaway with you. It's a relaxed and pleasant experience that embodies Savannah's pet-friendly spirit.

7.9 Blessing of the Pets: For a touching and spiritual experience, attend the Blessing of the Pets ceremony. Held at various churches and places of worship in Savannah, this event invites pet owners to bring their beloved furry companions for a special blessing. It's a touching and one-of-a-kind opportunity to celebrate the link between animals and their humans while also receiving offerings for their well-being.

So, fellow animal lover, there you have it - Savannah's hidden gems in the world of animal events! From the paw-some fun of the Woof Gang Bakery Doggie Carnival to the cherished Blessing of the Pets ceremony, these local traditions provide insight into the endearing bond shared by Savannah residents and their animal companions. Embrace the joy, share the love, and make memories that will warm your heart for years to come. Happy days, and may your Savannah animal adventures be filled with never-ending purrs and wagging tails!

Are you ready to create memories that will reignite your devotion to the animal kingdom? Then come along with us as we explore the wonderful world of Savannah's wildlife! Woof woof.

Chapter 8

Culinary Delights

Thanks for coming to Savannah, where your taste buds are going to get spoiled! This chapter is going to dive into the delectable realm of culinary delights that this quaint Southern city has to offer. While examining these delightful selections, you might notice that certain dining establishments have already been covered in other areas of this guide. Given that these culinary marvels are so extraordinary, they deserve to be highlighted in numerous chapters!

Prepare to go on a delicious trip that will leave you wanting even more, from noteworthy Southern comfort food to exquisite seafood and scrumptious local delicacies. Savannah's culinary culture promises to satisfy your every food craving, whether you're a foodie hunting for intriguing cuisines or a traveler looking for a chance to indulge oneself in the local delicacies.

At popular restaurants like Mrs. Wilkes' Dining Room, where family-style meals bring people together in the spirit of fellowship and good food, enjoy the homey aromas of the South with classic savory dishes. At The Grey or The Wyld Dock Bar, where coastal cuisine meets contemporary artistry, savor the freshness of the sea with amazing seafood offerings.

Remember to sweeten your visit with must-try local goodies like Savannah Bee Company's delectable pralines and gourmet honey. These sweets capture the essence of Savannah's culinary heritage and will leave you with a delicious recollection of your stay. So, get your tummy ready for an astonishing voyage through Savannah's delicacies, and get ready to savor the amazingly delicious marvels that make this city a food lover's paradise.

Did You Know? Savannah's culinary scene is a delectable fusion of Southern comfort food, coastal delights, and must-try local treats that will have your taste buds dancing joyfully? Let's take a savory journey through the hidden gems of Savannah's culinary delights, where each dish celebrates the city's rich history and diverse flavors.

8.1 Southern Comfort Food: Get ready to savor the inviting flavors of the South. Savannah is well-known for its hearty cuisine that both warms the heart and delights the palette. Mrs. Wilkes' Dining Room is an essential visit for an authentic Southern feast. For generations, this family-style restaurant has been a local institution, serving a daily menu of traditional Southern classics.

Every meal, from fried chicken and collard greens to buttery mashed potatoes and cornbread, is a work of love. Expect to share a table with other foodies, as dining at Mrs. Wilkes' is a collaborative experience that cultivates connections and companionship. Mrs. Wilkes' Dining Room is located at 107 West Jones Street, Savannah, Georgia 31401.

While Southern comfort food is a Savannah mainstay, did you know that Gullah Geechee culture plays a significant impact on the city's culinary heritage? Gullah

Geechee cuisine, a fusion of West African, European, and Native American culture, has left an indelible imprint on the cuisine of the region. Soul cuisine favorites like collard greens, crispy fried chicken, and flavorful seafood gumbo can be found at popular restaurants like Sisters of the New South and Sweet Potatoes Kitchen. While enjoying each delicious bite, absorb the historical and cultural diversity.

8.2 Seafood and Coastal Cuisine: Savannah takes its seafood seriously as a coastal city, and you're in for a seafood extravaganza! Head to The Grey, for a taste of elevated coastal cuisine featuring many seafood dishes, including succulent crab cakes, tender grilled octopus, and luscious shrimp and grits.

Another seafood gem is The Wyld Dock Bar, offering picturesque waterfront views and a laid-back atmosphere. Delight your taste buds with fresh catches like oysters, shrimp, and fish, while savoring the beauty of the coastal marsh. The Grey can be found in Savannah, Georgia at 109 Martin Luther King Jr. Boulevard, Savannah, GA 31401, and The Wyld Dock Bar is located at 2740 Livingston Ave, Savannah, GA 31406.

Beyond the famous riverfront restaurants, Savannah boasts hidden seafood gems that delight locals and astound visitors. Sample the succulent shrimp and grits, buttery crab cakes, and divine oysters, all locally sourced and prepared with passion. You'll discover that Savannah's love for seafood goes beyond the traditional coastal offerings, inviting you to embark on a flavorful seafood journey like no other.

8.3 Must-Try Local Treats: Don't leave Savannah without satisfying your sweet tooth with local treats! Make a beeline to the Savannah Bee Company, where you can sample some of the best pralines and gourmet honey in town. The Savannah Bee Company is another hidden gem where you can sample gourmet honey and honeycomb treats. Their tantalizing honey varieties, like Tupelo and Sourwood, make for unique souvenirs that capture the essence of Savannah's sweet and buzzing charm.

And when it comes to honey, Savannah Bee Company offers a wide variety of artisanal honey sourced from different floral regions. Each honey variety's distinct qualities can be tasted, making it a memorable and educational experience. The Savannah Bee Company has several locations in Savannah, including 104 W Broughton St, Savannah, GA 31401.

Indulging in Savannah's local treats is a must, and pralines are a sweet Southern delight you shouldn't miss. The Savannah Candy Kitchen is one of the go-to spots for these caramelized pecan confections. Did you know that these delectable pralines are made from butter, sugar, and pecans, offering a delightful blend of nutty and sweet flavors?

Savannah's culinary scene celebrates tradition and innovation, blending Southern heritage with coastal delights. From savoring Southern comfort food to relishing the finest seafood dishes, your taste buds are in for an unforgettable adventure. So, prepare your appetite for an incredible journey through the flavors of Savannah, and get ready to savor the culinary delights that make this city a food lover's paradise!

And we need to include this - River Street is one of the prime destinations for a diverse culinary experience in Savannah. This iconic cobblestone-lined street along the Savannah River is a food lover's paradise, boasting many dining options catering to every palate.

8.4 Food with a Side of History: The Pirates' House: While the Pirates' House has an excellent and unique history dating back to the 1700s, did you know that it's not just a restaurant but also a fascinating museum? As one of the oldest standing buildings in Georgia, this iconic establishment serves up delectable Southern dishes amidst its historic charm. Enjoy a meal in the spot where pirates and sailors once gathered, and explore the Pirate House Museum for a glimpse into Savannah's swashbuckling past.

8.5 River Street Eateries: River Street is a gourmet tapestry of varied cuisines as well as a lovely pathway along the riverbanks! Discover local favorites like Huey's On The River, which serves scrumptious beignets and Southern-style breakfasts with a view, in addition to the famous seafood restaurants. Do you want some spice and soul? Dub's Pub offers a memorable experience with its Cajun-inspired menu and rooftop dining. River Street's dining options are a medley of flavors that pay tribute to Savannah's culinary heart.

River Street offers a wide variety of dishes that represent the city's rich cultural diversity. Fresh catches from the ocean, such as juicy shrimp, crispy fish and chips, and savory seafood platters, are available to seafood fans. There are numerous seafood restaurants and eateries, each offering a twist on coastal cuisine.

Southern Flavors:

For a taste of true Southern comfort, River Street boasts charming restaurants that serve up classic serve up familiar dishes like fried chicken, collard greens, and shrimp and grits. Savor the mouthwatering flavors passed down through generations, providing a warm and nostalgic dining experience.

International Cuisine:

River Street is also a haven for those seeking a taste of international fare. From Mexican and Italian to Asian and Mediterranean, you'll find a delightful array of global flavors that showcase Savannah's diverse culinary scene.

Sweet Treats:

Remember to indulge your sweet tooth with the abundance of sweet treats on River Street. From artisanal chocolates and gourmet ice cream to freshly baked pastries and pralines, there's something to satisfy every sugar craving.

Scenic Dining Experience:

As you enjoy your meal, take in the picturesque views of the Savannah River, watching ships sail by and feeling the gentle breeze. The riverfront ambiance adds an extra touch of magic to your dining experience, making it an unforgettable moment in your journey.

Food Festivals and Events:

Keep an eye out for exceptional food festivals and events that often take place on River Street. These gatherings showcase the best local and regional culinary delights, allowing you to taste a wide-array of unique flavors in one place.

So, whether you're strolling along River Street for a scenic meal by the river, indulging in the diverse culinary offerings, or exploring the unique food festivals, this historic street is a must-visit destination for any food lover. Embrace the flavors of Savannah and immerse yourself in the vibrant culinary scene that makes this city a true delight for foodies!

So, foodie friend, there you have it - Savannah's food surprises, with a few twists thrown in! Each meal is a culinary adventure that intertwines history, culture, and sheer deliciousness, from the soulful flavors of Gullah Geechee cuisine to the yummy enticement of Savannah's sweet delicacies. Immerse yourself in the rich tapestry of sensations and let your taste buds go on an unforgettable dining voyage. Bon appétit, and may your Savannah food experience be nothing short of amazing!

Chapter 9

———

Accommodations and Lodging

It's time to unwind and refuel for more activities in Savannah! In this chapter, we're going to take a look at hotels and lodging options that will satisfy the demands of any visitor. But, before we dive into the gorgeous places to stay, let's talk about one of Savannah's most treasured features of culture: its famous Southern hospitality.

The graciousness and kindness of the South will take hold of you from the moment you arrive in Savannah. Savannahians have an uncanny ability to make you feel like an old friend returning home, and their real kindness shines through in every connection. It's not uncommon for innkeepers to greet you with warm grins and treat you as if you were a valued visitor in their house. It's not uncommon for innkeepers to greet you with warm grins and treat you as if you were a valued visitor in their house. Whether you stay in a historic inn or a luxurious hotel, you'll be steeped in the atmosphere of Southern hospitality that characterizes this charming city.

Throughout your stay, you'll notice the small details that make an enormous difference, such as pleasant conversations with locals at breakfast and helpful tips for discovering hidden gems. Expect individual attention and hospitality that will make your stay in Savannah feel like more than simply a journey; it will be a once-in-a-lifetime experience.

As we investigate Savannah's various housing and lodging alternatives, we're going to find that the true hospitality of the city's citizens goes beyond its historical core and easily flows into the hospitality of its lodging options. So, get ready to be embraced by the true spirit of Southern charm as we wander through the beautiful facilities that are sure to improve your Savannah experience. Let's find the ideal place to unwind and refresh, surrounded by Savannah's famed Southern hospitality.

Did You Know? Savannah's accommodations and lodging options offer more than just a place to rest your head; they're a gateway to the city's captivating history and Southern charm? Let's dive into the hidden gems of Savannah's lodging scene, where each stay becomes a unique experience that immerses you in the heart of this enchanting city.

9.1 Historic Inns and B&Bs: Staying at one of Savannah's historic inns or a quaint bed and breakfast is a must if you're interested in the city's rich history and appearance. These charming rooms provide a one-of-a-kind experience, bringing you back to the days of gracious Southern hospitality. Envision waking up in a magnificently renovated mansion, complete with antique furnishings and historical decor.

The innkeepers' special focus adds a touch of warmth, making you feel like an honored guest in their house. Every morning, enjoy an excellently prepared breakfast before discovering the city's historic treasures. These accommodations, with their excellent locations near the charming squares and architectural wonders, make it easy to immerse yourself in Savannah's captivating environment.

While Savannah's historic inns and bed and breakfasts are well-known for their charm, did you know that some of these hidden jewels have fascinating stories to tell as well as intriguing histories? Stay at the Kehoe home, which used to be a magnificent estate turned boarding house, and you might run into a friendly spirit of a long-gone occupant! Alternatively, Azalea Inn & Villas, a renovated 19th-century mansion with secret gardens and a great afternoon tea experience, offers elegance. These historic bed and breakfasts provide more than just a nice place to stay; they welcome you to become a part of Savannah's rich tapestry of history.

9.2 Luxury Hotels: Savannah's luxury hotels are sure to exceed your expectations for those seeking indulgence and modern comforts. These top-rated establishments offer a world-class experience that pampers you from the moment you step through the doors. Imagine elegant rooms with plush bedding and upscale amenities, providing the perfect sanctuary after a day of exploration.

Many Savannah luxury hotels have gorgeous rooftop bars or lounges with stunning views of the city or riverside. Exquisite dining experiences await you at the hotel's famed restaurants, where professional chefs create culinary marvels using the best ingredients. Relax at the hotel's spa, get a relaxing massage, and drink in the sophistication that surrounds you.

Savannah has numerous magnificent hideaways where modern comfort meets fascinating pasts aside from the city's top luxury hotels. Did you know that The Mansion on Forsyth Park has luxurious amenities and a large art collection, making it a refuge for art lovers? Also, don't miss the Perry Lane Hotel, where sophisticated design meets Southern hospitality, with rooftop views and an artistic atmosphere. These luxurious escapes are more than just accommodations; they invite you to indulge in the grandeur of Savannah's past while relishing every modern luxury.

Recommended Locations:

· **Historic Inns and B&Bs:** Check out the Olde Harbour Inn (508 E Factors Walk, Savannah, GA 31401) to blend history and modern comforts. The Kehoe House (123 Habersham St, Savannah, GA 31401) is another elegant choice with its inviting verandas and grand architecture.

· **Luxury Hotels:** The Perry Lane Hotel (256 E Perry St, Savannah, GA 31401) offers a luxurious urban retreat with stylish decor and stunning city views. For a riverfront experience, consider The Riverfront Bohemian Hotel in Savannah (102 W Bay St, Savannah, GA 31401) with its chic ambiance and excellent dining options.

Choosing the proper accommodation for your Savannah adventure is critical for having a memorable and pleasurable stay. Whether you prefer the elegance of historical inns or the lavish amenities of luxury hotels, each option guarantees a one-of-a-kind experience that will leave you with pleasant memories of your time in this fantastic Southern city. Rest assured, Savannah offers the ideal location to meet your needs and make your stay nothing short of exceptional. Wishing you happiness and safe travels!

9.3 Charming Historic District Boutiques: Tucked away in the Historic District, charming boutique hotels offer a local experience like no other. Check in to The Marshall House (123 E Broughton St, Savannah, GA 31401), Savannah's oldest hotel, where exposed brick walls and vintage charm create a romantic atmosphere. Or venture to The Gastonian (220 E Gaston St, Savannah, GA 31401), a pair of Federal-style townhouses with lush gardens and gourmet breakfasts, a dreamy escape for couples seeking romance. These boutique gems provide an intimate and personalized stay, making you feel like a cherished guest in the heart of Savannah's history.

9.4 Hidden Riverfront Retreats on the Water's Edge: Though Savannah's riverfront is often brimming with activity, did you know it also has calm and secret retreats? The Riverfront Bohemian Hotel in Savannah (102 W Bay St, Savannah, GA 31401) has spectacular river views and an exciting rooftop lounge. Or, for waterfront luxury, visit The Westin Golf Resort & Spa at Savannah Harbor (1 Resort Dr, Savannah, GA 31421), where you could play golf and enjoy a refreshing spa treatment with spectacular river views. These secret riverfront havens allow you to enjoy the tranquillity of the river while staying only a few steps away from the lively activity of the city.

So there you have it, fellow travelers: Savannah's hidden treasures in the field of lodgings and housing! Every stay is an opportunity to become a part of Savannah's fascinating history, from the intriguing tales about historical inns to the splendor of secret luxury hotels. Embrace the charm, embrace the history, and let your Savannah hotel experience transport you to an alternate universe where comfort meets traditions from the past. Sweet dreams, and may your Savannah vacation be filled with unforgettable memories!

Chapter 10

When to Visit Savannah

Savannah's seasons have a considerable impact on visitors' decisions about when to visit and experience the city's charms. Each season has its own atmosphere as well as events that cater to different tastes and interests. Let's take a closer look at how the time of year could influence travelers' decisions.

Hot Tip: As you embark on a journey through time, you'll find that each season adds a special touch to the city's enchanting squares and architectural wonders. Each season offers a unique atmosphere and activities, catering to different preferences and interests. Let's take a closer look at how the seasons affect visitors' choices:

Spring:

The Historic District comes alive with vivid colors and flowering azaleas as the first warm breeze blows through the city. Spring is the ideal season for a leisurely stroll through the squares, with its residents and visitors alike picnicking under the blossoming trees. The scent of flowers permeates the air as you stroll through the Owens-Thomas House's beautiful garden. Take advantage of the yearly Savannah Tour of Mansions and Gardens, where you can go inside private historic mansions and get a firsthand look at the district's magnificence.

(**March to May**): Savannah comes alive in the spring with colorful blooms and nice weather, making it an enchanting time to visit. Azaleas, magnolias, and wisteria color the town, providing a gorgeous setting for leisurely strolls through old squares and gardens. The warm temperatures, which typically range from the 60s to the 70s Fahrenheit (15°C to 25°C), make it suitable for outdoor activities such as walking tours, bike rides, and viewing the city's sights without being too hot like in the summer. Spring also heralds the start of festival season, with events such as the Savannah Music Festival and the Savannah Tour of Homes and Gardens bringing tourists from all over.

Summer:

Summer in Savannah is a time for leisurely days and sipping sweet tea. Why? Because it is extremely hot! Despite the heat, the Historic District's rich foliage and shaded squares provide a welcome relief. Enjoy the city's beauty while staying cool by going on a leisurely carriage ride. As the sun sets, join residents for Music in the Squares, where live acts provide a musical backdrop to your wanderings. For a one-of-a-kind summer experience, head to Forsyth Park for Shakespeare in the Park, where the Bard's masterpieces are brought to life under the stars.

(**June to August**): Summers in Savannah tend to be hot and humid, with highs in the 90s Fahrenheit (32°C) with afternoon thunderstorms. Summer is a wonderful season to see the city's buzzing vitality for visitors who appreciate a dynamic atmosphere and wish to take advantage of the longer daylight hours. You may beat the heat by drinking a cool beverage from one of the many ice cream shops or sampling a mint julep. Better yet, stop by Wet Willies for a refreshing frozen adult beverage! While outdoor activities may cause some forethought to escape the noon heat, you can still enjoy water-based excursions, harbor cruises, and leisurely riverboat rides. Summer also brings with it a number of events, such as the Fourth of July celebrations and Savannah's Seafood Festival.

Fall:

The Historic District embraces the beginning of the autumn season with open arms when the temperature drops. The oak trees begin to turn fall colors, offering a lovely backdrop for your travels. Make plans to attend the Savannah Jazz Festival, which takes place in Forsyth Park and features toe-tapping rhythms and seductive tunes. Take a ghost tour through the district for a taste of eerie enjoyment, as the city's ghostly tales become even more captivating during the Halloween season.

(**September to November**): Fall is well-known for attracting travelers looking for cooler temperatures and less crowds. The humidity begins to decrease, and the temperature jumps into the 70s and 80s Fahrenheit (20°C to 30°C). The city's gardens and parks continue to provide a spectacular display of autumn color, making it an ideal time for nature lovers and photographers. The Savannah Film Festival, which attracts cinephiles and movie enthusiasts from all over the world, also returns in the fall. Fall is an exciting season to see Savannah's cultural scene and appreciate the city's artistic personality, with a variety of outdoor celebrations and gatherings.

Winter:

Winter adds a festive touch to the Historic District. During the Holiday Tour of Homes, festive lights embrace the squares, and the aroma of roasted chestnuts fills the air. Stroll amid the dazzling lights of the Savannah Harbor Holiday Series, where you can ice skate and even see Santa. Attend the annual Savannah Christmas Parade for a really memorable event, as local marching bands, floats, and Santa himself create a cheerful setting.

(**December to February**): Savannah's winters are warm, with temperatures ranging from the 50s to the 60s Fahrenheit (10°C to 20°C). While the city may not receive much snow, holiday decorations adorning historic buildings and squares provide a touch of winter elegance. Winter is a good time for budget-conscious tourists because hotel rates are lower than during busy tourist seasons. Savannah features a variety of holiday activities, including the iconic St. Patrick's Day festival, which draws visitors from all over the world. Assuming you want a more private and intimate setting, winter allows you to avoid crowds and explore the city's sites and museums.

Year-Round Charm:

The Historic District's ageless charm never fades, no matter the season. Its cobblestone pathways and exquisite buildings provide a picturesque setting for carriage excursions and leisurely strolls. While exploring the district, stop into local boutiques and art galleries that feature the work of great Savannah artists. Make time to see the Historic Savannah Theatre, the country's oldest continuously operating theater, where you can catch vibrant shows all year.

So, whether you're looking for the vivid blooms of spring, the Southern charm of summer, the colorful glory of fall, or the festive magic of winter, the Historic District has something for you in every season.

Finally, the optimum time to visit Savannah depends on your particular interests and whatever activities you desire to participate in during your stay. Savannah welcomes you with its characteristic Southern hospitality all year round, whether you favor the flowering beauty of spring, the bustling energy of summer, the brilliant foliage of fall, or the milder winters. So, choose the season that speaks to your spirit and prepare for a memorable journey in this amazing city!

Chapter 11

Conclusion

Congratulations on tackling your Savannah to-do list! Did you finish it? If you didn't, don't worry; you now have another reason to return and work on it later, lol! We hope your visit to this fascinating city was a great trip packed with rich history, vibrant culture, and scrumptious flavors that truly characterize the soul of the South. As we say goodbye to this charming place, allow us to stop and enjoy and treasure the unforgettable experiences you've enjoyed in Savannah.

Savannah's Historic Treasures:

You've walked through Savannah's lovely squares and historic structures, which tell the story of the city's past. Each step transported you through a time warp, immersing you in the lush greenery of Forsyth Park, the peaceful calm of Lafayette Square, and the awe-inspiring Gothic architecture of the Cathedral of St. John the Baptist. With its moss-covered tombstones whispering stories of bygone times, the hauntingly beautiful Bonaventure Cemetery gripped your attention with its beauty.

River Street and Culinary Delights:

River Street became your culinary playground, where you sampled mouthwatering seafood dishes, nibbled on tasty sweet treats, and savored delectable Southern comfort food. The tantalizing aroma of freshly baked pralines filled the air, and you couldn't resist taking a few extra treats home to savor the sweet flavors of Savannah even after your journey was over.

Adventure on Savannah's Islands:

Beyond the lovely streets of Savannah, you can explore the calm of Tybee Island's sandy shoreline and the spectacular panoramas of Skidaway Island State Park's nature trails. The Dolphin Watching Tours got you up close and personal with playful marine life, filling you with awe and respect for Savannah's coastal splendor.

Sporting Events and Festivals:

Your Savannah journey was alive with excitement as you cheered on the Savannah Bananas at Grayson Stadium and raced in the Rock 'n' Roll Marathon. Attending the Savannah Music Festival and other dynamic cultural events immersed you in the vivid spirit of the city, connecting you with both locals and fellow travelers by means of mutual joyful celebrations.

Southern Hospitality and Ideal Seasons:

You were embraced by the real warmth of Southern hospitality throughout your journey, making you feel like an honored guest in Savannah's welcoming arms. You explored the city across multiple seasons and found out that each season has its own distinct beauty. Savannah displayed its beauty in all four seasons, from the brilliant blooms of spring to the magnificent holiday lights of winter.

As you say goodbye to Savannah, we hope the memories of its moss-draped trees, historical treasures, and lively atmosphere linger with you for the rest of your life. Let the charm of this wonderful city linger in your heart, encouraging you to return for another thrilling adventure. When you resume on your adventure, keep in mind that the soul of Savannah is to be found not just in its landmarks, but also in the people you meet, the foods that you sample, and the excitement of discovery that permeates every moment of your stay.

Until we meet again, may your future travels be filled with wonder, curiosity, and the thrill of finding new places to explore. Best wishes, my friend! Happy travels, dear friend!

SSS. :)

Don't miss out!

Visit the website below and you can sign up to receive emails whenever Susyn S. Shepherd publishes a new book. There's no charge and no obligation.

https://books2read.com/r/B-A-IMVZ-GMNMC

BOOKS2READ

Connecting independent readers to independent writers.